Learn to Sing Harmony

Homespun Learning Discs — 3 CDs

taught by
Cathy Fink, Marcy Marxer,
Robin and Linda Williams

Cover photo by Adam Traum

ISBN 0-63404-482-6

Homespun Tapes

©1989 and 1998 Homespun Tapes, Ltd.
Box 340
Woodstock, NY 12498
All Rights Reserved

No part of this publication may be reproduced in any form or by any means
without the prior written permission of the Publisher.

Visit Homespun Tapes on the internet at
www.homespuntapes.com

Learn To Sing Harmony
taught by
Cathy Fink, Marcy Marxer, Robin and Linda Williams

CD - One

Track
1   intro and series overview

Basics of harmony
2   the melody
3   major scale
4   intervals
5   learning intervals (ear training)
6   interval talk
7   two notes at once
8   harmony and chord structure
9   finding the harmony

Down By The Riverside
10   talk
11   melody played in C
12   with higher harmony in C
13   with lower harmony in E

Bury Me Beneath The Willow
14   with harmony in C
15   with harmony in D

Red River Valley
16   with harmony (high) in C
17   with harmony (low) in F#

Long Journey Home
18   in D
19   in G

Mountain Dew
20   (chorus) in D
21   (chorus) in G

Hand Me Down My Walking Cane
22   in C
23   in G

CD - Two

Track

1   intro

Careless Love
2   talk
3   in G
4   in C
5   in D
6   creating a blend/phrasing

Trouble In Mind
7   talk
8   played in D
9   breakdown
10   in G

Leavin' Train
11   in A
12   independent movement

Down In The Valley
13   talk
14   in G
15   in E

Turtle Dove
16   talk
17   in B$\flat$
18   breakdown
19   parallel fourths
20   key changes

Little Darlin' Pal Of Mine
21   talk
22   played

CD - Three

Track	
1	intro and overview

Gold Watch And Chain
2	played
3	building three-part harmony
4	melody sung
5	melody & harmony (below) sung
6	melody & harmony (above) sung
7	three parts sung
8	three parts sung in D
9	melody sung in D
10	melody & harmony (above) in D
11	melody & harmony (below) in D
12	three parts sung in D

Keep On The Sunny Side
13	played
14	melody sung in C
15	melody and 1st harmony sung in C
16	melody and 2nd harmony sung in C
17	all parts sung in C
18	sung in G
19	melody sung in G
20	melody and 1st harmony sung in G
21	melody and 2nd harmony sung in G
22	all parts sung in G

Blues Stay Away From Me
23	talk
24	all parts in A
25	melody
26	chords sung
27	melody and 1st harmony
28	melody and 2nd harmony
29	melody and bass
30	melody and bass variations
31	all parts full versions

Amazing Grace
32	talk
33	all parts (one verse)
34	melody
35	melody and (high) harmony
36	melody and (low) harmony
37	melody and bass
38	all parts (complete version)

(CD - Three continued)

Goodnight, Irene
39	talk
40	all parts (one chorus)
41	melody
42	melody and (low) harmony
43	melody and (high) harmony
44	melody and bass
45	all parts (complete version)
46	harmony talk

Stay All Night
47	all parts

Learn to Sing Harmony
CD 1

Contents

Basics of Harmony	3
Down By The Riverside	5
Bury Me Beneath The Willow	7
Red River Valley	9
Long Journey Home	10
Good Old Mountain Dew	11
Hand Me Down My Walking Cane	12
Additional song lyrics	13

Basics of Harmony

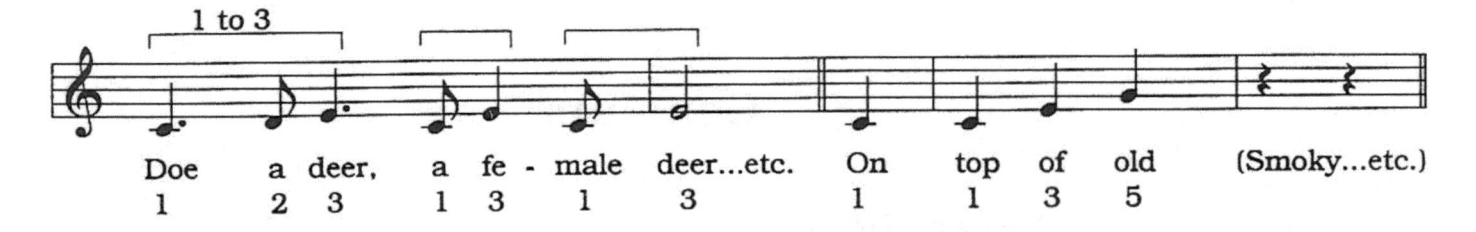

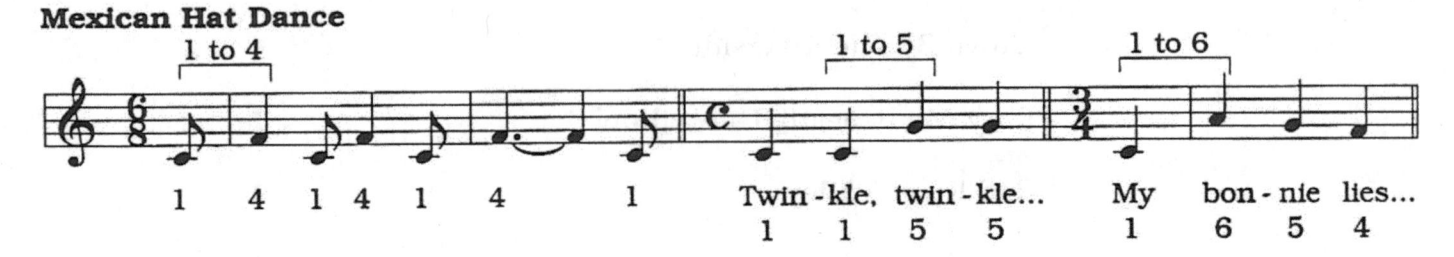

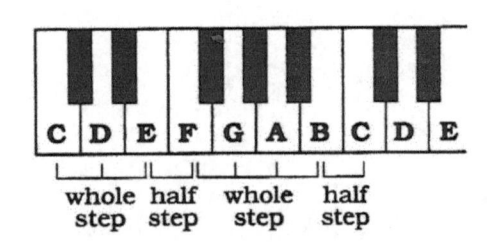

Basics of Harmony

Here are some elementary definitions that you will need to know:

A *half step*: The interval between one note and the next closest note, either up or down. For example, a half step up from C would be C#; a half step down would be B.

A *whole step* consists of two half steps either up or down from the original note. For example, a whole step up from C would be D; a whole step down from C would be Bb.

A *major scale* is made up of the following formula of whole steps and half steps: whole, whole, half, whole, whole, whole, half.

A *chord* is made up of three (or more) notes heard simultaneously. The most common chord is made up of a *major triad* consisting of the 1st (or *root*), the 3rd, and the 5th tones of a major scale. The major triad of the C scale is C (1), E (3), and G (5). These notes may be played or sung in any order, or *inversion*.

Look at the diagram of a keyboard on the previous page (or better yet, look at a real keyboard) and get familiar with half steps and whole steps, and how they form a scale. The C scale naturally falls in the right formula on the white keys. Other keys must make use of sharps or flats (black keys) to arrive at the correct combination of steps to make a major scale.

All of the demonstrations of intervals on the CDs are in relation to the root, or (1) of each key, although you can use any other starting note as well. For instance, in the key of C, the notes G to B ("5" to "7") is a third. In the key of G, G becomes the root or "1" and B is the 3rd note in the scale ("3") but the interval is still a 3rd.

Although the intervals on the CDs are heard in the keys of C and G, they are only written out in this booklet in C. Use your ear to *transpose* or change keys.

Harmony singing is a joyful experience. It often makes a song feel fuller and stronger, and when done well makes both singers and listeners feel good. This basic instruction method will help you train your ear to hear different harmony intervals and parts. Learn the songs that we teach on these CDs using your ear as much as possible. If you get stuck you can plunk out the written parts on a piano or guitar. The first lesson should give you a basic understanding of the theory behind harmony singing, although it is by no means comprehensive. For further study in ear training and theory, we recommend Matt Glaser's series "Ear Training for Instrumentalists" on Homespun Tapes.

We hope you have a great deal of fun listening to these CDs, and singing along with them.

In harmony,

Cathy, Linda, Marcy, Robin

Down By The Riverside

Melody – lower line, harmony – upper line

I'm gon-na lay down my sword and shield down by the ri-ver-side. Down by the ri-ver-side, down by the ri-ver-side. I'm gon-na lay down my sword and shield down by the ri-ver-side, stu-dy war no more. I ain't gon-na stu-dy war no more, I ain't gon-na stu-dy war no more, I ain't gon-na stu-dy war no more, I ain't gon-na stu-dy war no more, ain't gon-na stu-dy war no more.

Down By The Riverside

Melody – upper line

I'm gon-na lay down my sword and shield down by the ri-ver-side. Down by the ri-ver-side, down by the ri-ver-side, I'm gon-na lay down my sword and shield down by the ri-ver-side, Stu-dy war no more. I ain't gon-na stu-dy war no more, I ain't gon-na stu-dy war no more, I ain't gonna stu-dy war no more, I ain't gon-na stu-dy war no more, I ain't gon-na stu-dy war no more, ain't gon-na stu-dy war no more.

Bury Me Beneath The Willow

Melody – lower line, harmony – upper line

My heart is sad and I am lone - ly,
Think - ing of the one I love, When will I
see him. Oh, no ne - ver Unless we meet in heav'n a -
bove. So bu - ry me be - neath the
wil - low, Un - der the weep - ing wil - low tree,
So he may know where I am
sleep - ing, Then per - haps he'll think of me.

Bury Me Beneath The Willow

Melody – lower line, harmony – upper line

My heart is sad and I am lone-ly, Thinking of the one I love, When will I see him, Oh, no ne-ver Unless we meet in heav'n a-bove. So bu-ry me be-neath the wil-low, Under the weeping wil-low tree, So he may know where I am sleeping, Then per-haps he'll think of me.

Red River Valley

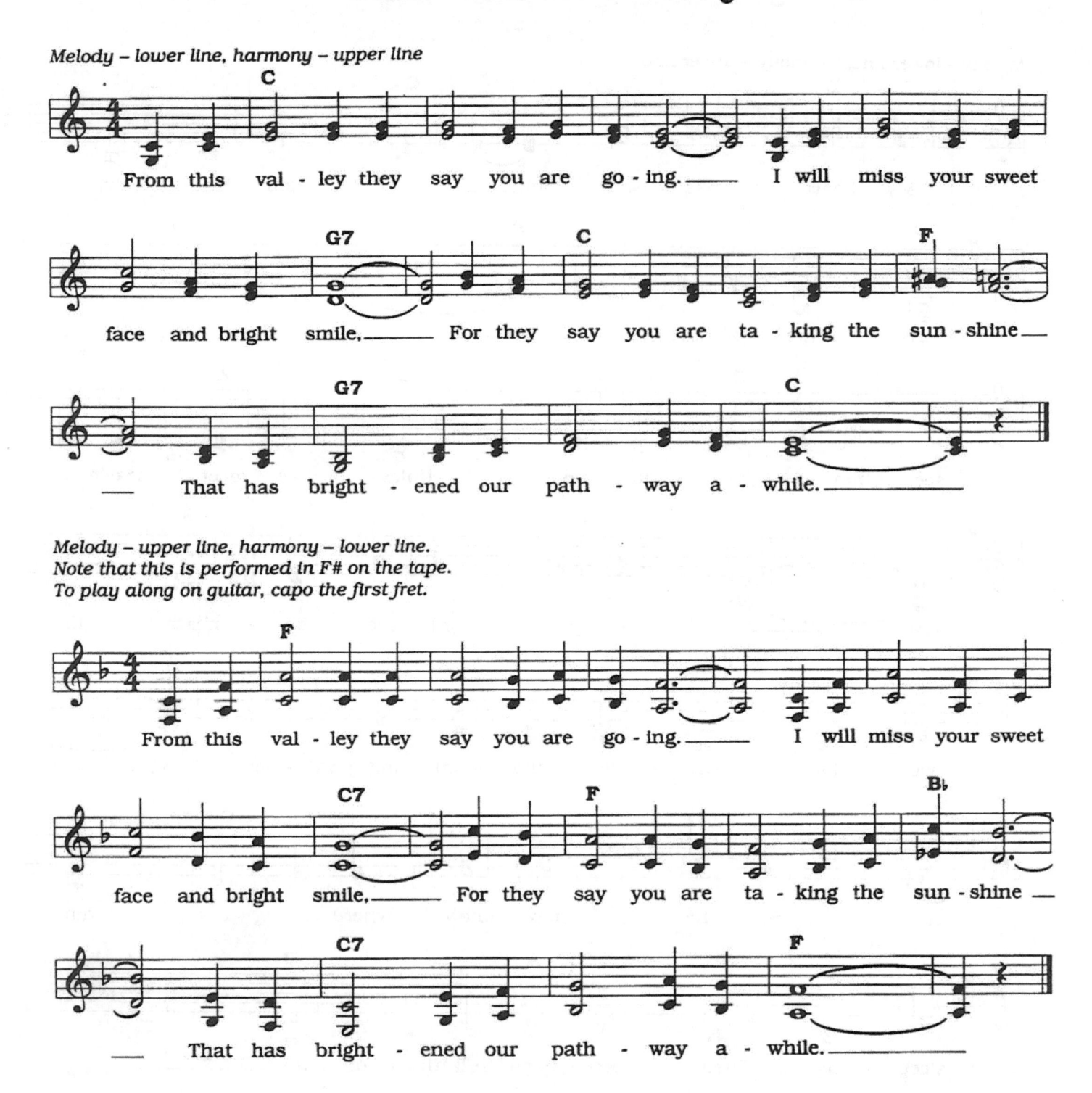

Melody – lower line, harmony – upper line

From this valley they say you are going. I will miss your sweet face and bright smile, For they say you are taking the sunshine That has brightened our pathway awhile.

Melody – upper line, harmony – lower line.
Note that this is performed in F# on the tape.
To play along on guitar, capo the first fret.

From this valley they say you are going. I will miss your sweet face and bright smile, For they say you are taking the sunshine That has brightened our pathway awhile.

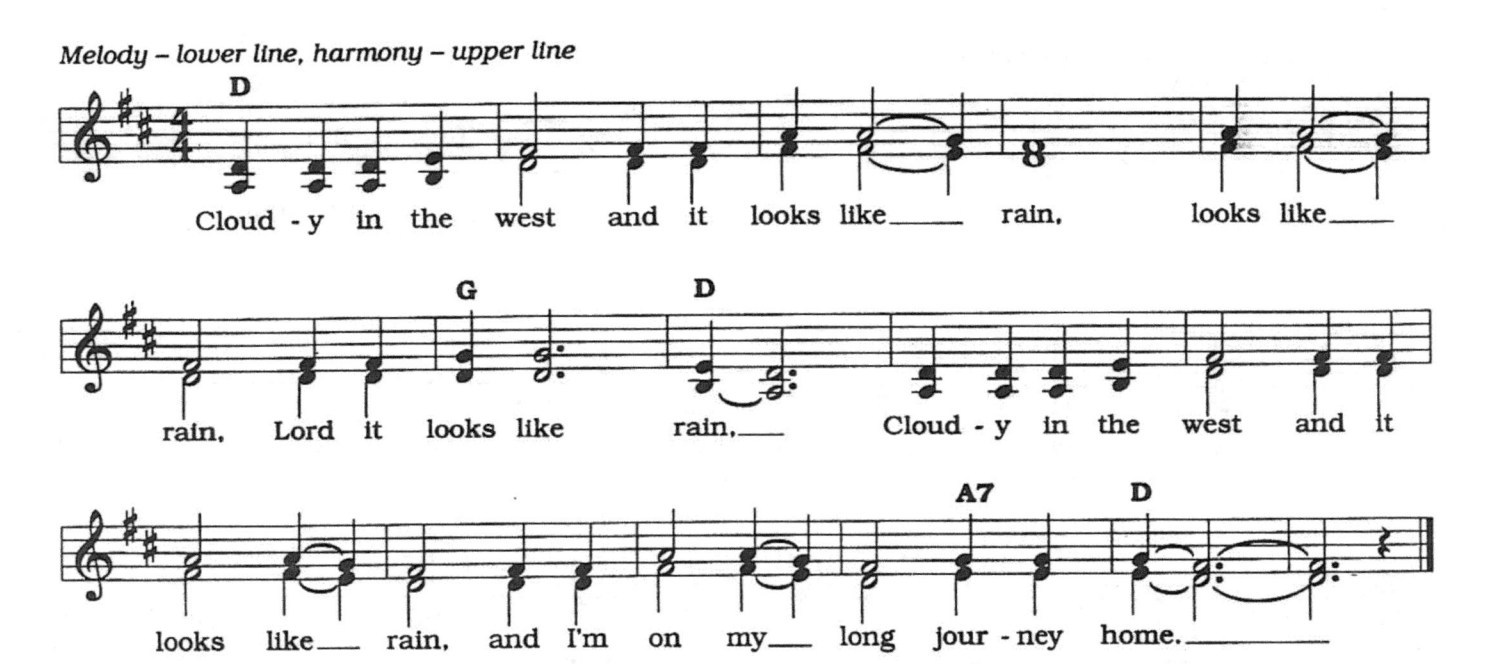

Long Journey Home

Melody – lower line, harmony – upper line

Cloud-y in the west and it looks like rain, looks like rain, Lord it looks like rain, Cloud-y in the west and it looks like rain, and I'm on my long jour-ney home.

Melody – upper line, harmony – lower line

Cloud-y in the west and it looks like rain, looks like rain, Lord it looks like rain. Cloud-y in the west and it looks like rain, and I'm on my long jour-ney home.

Mountain Dew

Melody – lower line, harmony – upper line

They call it that good old moun-tain dew, _____ and them that re-fuse it are few. _____ Now, hush up your mug and fill up your jug with that good old _____ moun-tain dew. _____

Melody – upper line

They call it that good old moun-tain dew. _____ and them that re-fuse it are few. _____ Now, hush up your mug and fill up your jug with that good old _____ moun-tain dew. _____

Hand Me Down My Walking Cane

Melody – top line

Hand me down my walk-ing cane, Oh, hand me down my walk-ing cane, Hand me down my walk-ing cane, I'm gon-na catch the mid-night train, All my sins are tak-en a-way.

Melody – lower line

Hand me down my walk-ing cane, Oh hand me down my walk-ing cane, Hand me down my walk-ing cane, I'm gon-na catch the mid-night train. All my sins are tak-en a way.

SONG LYRICS

Bury Me Beneath The Willow

Verse 2:

He told me that he dearly loved me,
How could I believe it untrue,
Until the day some neighbors told me
He has proven untrue to you.

Red River Valley

(Verse and chorus are the same melody)

Chorus:

Come and sit by my side e'er you leave me,
Do not hasten to bid me adieu,
But remember the Red River Valley,
And the cowgirl who loved you so true.

I have promised you darling that never
Will the words from my lips cause you pain,
And my life it will be yours forever
If you only will love me again.

Long Journey home

Lost all my money but a two dollar bill,
Two dollar bill, Lord, a two dollar bill,
Lost all my money but a two dollar bill,
And I'm on my long journey home.

Black smoke a-risin' and it surely is a train,
Surely is a train, Lord, surely is a train,
Black smoke a-risin' and it surely is a train,
And I'm on my long journey home.

Walking Cane

Additional verse:

Hand me down my bottle of corn (2x)
Hand me down my bottle of corn, I'll get
Drunk as sure as you're born,
All my sins are taken away.

Inscribed by CHARYLU ROBERTS

Learn to Sing Harmony
CD 2

Contents

Trouble In Mind	3
Down In The Valley	4
Careless Love	5
Turtle Dove	7
Leaving Train	11
Little Darlin' Pal Of Mine	12
Additional song lyrics	13

Trouble In Mind

Melody – upper line, harmony – lower line

Linda: Trou-ble in mind, I'm blue,___ But I won't be blue al-ways,___ The sun's gon-na shine___ in my back door___ some___ day.___

Robin: (harmony)

Melody – Lower line, harmony – upper line

Linda: Trou-ble in mind, I'm blue,___ But I won't be blue al-ways,___ The sun's gon-na shine___ in my back door___ some___ day.___

Robin: (harmony)

Down In The Valley

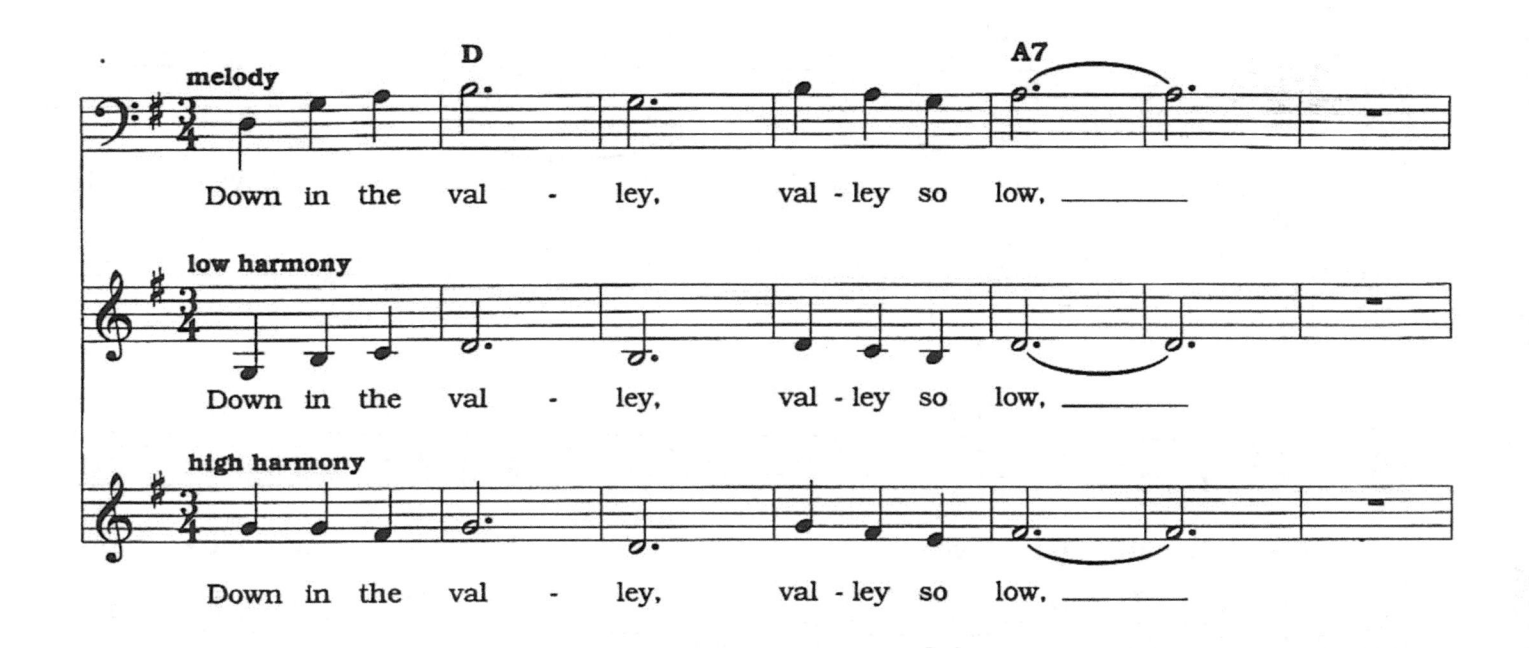

Careless Love

love, oh care-less love. Love, oh love, oh care-less love, See what care-less love has done.

Key of D

Love, oh love, oh care-less love. Love, oh love, oh care-less love, See what care-less love has done.

Turtle Dove

Tur-tle dove done drooped his wings. (Done drooped his wings.)

Tur-tle dove done drooped his wings, Tur-tle dove done drooped his wings,

High on Zi-on's Hill to sing. A-dam and Eve, Do, Do,

A-dam and Eve won't you tell it to me, Meet me at the door, won't you tell it to me?

meet me at the door, won't you tell it to me? Fa sa la sa do on sa la sa ree.

When I get to hea-ven I'll know the

(I'll know the rules.) When I get to hea-ven I'll know the rules.

When I get to hea-ven I'll know the rules.

Skip on down to the bath-ing pool. A-dam and Eve, do do

A-dam and Eve won't you tell it to me Meet me at the door, won't you tell it to me,

Fa sa la sa do on sa la sa ree. My

name is writ-ten on Da-vid's line. My
(On Dav-id's line.)

name is writ-ten on Da - vid's line. My
name is writ-ten on Da - vid's line. I'll go to hea-ven on the wheel of time.
A - dam and Eve, do, do. A - dam and Eve won't you tell it to me?
Meet me at the door won't you tell it to me? Fa sa la sa do on sa la sa ree.

Leaving Train

Words and Music by Linda H. Williams

Some-day soon I'm gon-na ride on the leav-in' train by ma-ma's side. There's a bro-ken link in the fam-'ly chain, and it's all be-cause of the leav-in' train. To feel her lov-in' touch when it's what I want so much. But one day I will go 'cause Ma-ma told me so.

Copyright © 1983 The New Music Times, Inc. (BMI)

Little Darlin' Pal Of Mine

Note: On tape this is sung in C#. To play with the tape, capo on first fret and play as written.

Oh, little darlin', Oh how I love you, How I love you none can tell. In your heart you love another. Little darlin' pal of mine.

There are just three things I wish for, Have my casket shroud in gray, When I'm dead don't dream o'er me, just kiss the lips that you betray.

SONG LYRICS

Trouble In Mind

2. I'm gonna lay my head on some lonesome railroad line
   And let the 2:19 ease my troubled mind.

3. Trouble in mind, I'm blue, my poor heart's beating slow,
   I ain't had so much trouble in my life before.

Down In The Valley

2. Hear the wind blow, dear, hear the wind blow.
   Hang your head over, hear the wind blow.

3. Roses love sunshine, violets love dew,
   Angels in heaven know I love you,
   Know I love you, dear, etc.

4. Write me a letter, send it by mail.
   Send it in care of Birmingham jail.
   Birmingham jail, love, etc.

Careless Love

2. I love my mama and papa too,
   I love my mama and papa too,
   I love my mama and papa too,
   I'd leave them both to go with you.

3. What, oh what, will mama say (3x),
   When she learns I've gone astray.

4. Once I wore my aprons low (3x),
   He'd follow me through ice and snow.

5. Now I wear my aprons high (3x),
   He sees my door and goes by.

Leaving Train

1. Mama's coming home today, but she ain't
      coming home to stay.
   There's no work in our town, everything's
      near about shut down.
   The company's come and gone, all the new
      folks moved on.
   Empty stores in empty streets, empty bed
      where Mama sleeps.

(Chorus)

2. When Friday comes I go back down to the
      train depot,
   She's running way behind and Sunday
      haunts my mind.
   It's been a week since the train stopped
      here, one week since she held me near.
   But too soon that leaving train will carry her
      off again.

3. Living without Mama hurts but I don't know
      which is worse;
   Her being gone way or having just one day
   To feel her loving touch when it's what I
      want so much,
   But someday I will go 'cause Mama told me
      so.

Little Darlin' Pal Of Mine

1. In the night while you lay sleeping,
   Dreaming of your amber skies
   Was a poor boy brokenhearted
   listening to the wind that cries.

(Chours)

2. Many's the day with you I rambled,
   Happiest hours with you I spent.
   Thought I had your love forever,
   But I find it's only lent.

(Chours)

3. There are just three things I wish for;
   Have my casket shroud in gray.
   When I'm dead, don't dream o'er me,
   Just kiss the lips that you betrayed.

Inscribed by **CHARYLU ROBERTS**

Learn to Sing Harmony
CD 3

Contents

Gold Watch And Chain	3
Keep On The Sunny Side	5
Blues Stay Away From Me	7
Amazing Grace	9
Irene Goodnight	11
Stay All Night	13
Additional song lyrics	14

Gold Watch And Chain

I will pawn you my gold watch and chain, love,— I will pawn you my gold— wed-ding ring. I will pawn you this heart in my bo-som,— On-ly say that you love— me a-gain.

Marcy (melody), Cathy, Robin

I will pawn you my gold watch and chain love, I will pawn you my gold wedding ring. I will pawn you this heart in my bosom. Only say that you love me again.

Keep On The Sunny Side

Keep on the sunny side always on the sunny side.

Keep on the sunny side of life. It will help us ev-'ry day, It will

bright-en all our way, If we keep on the sunny side of life.

Keep On The Sunny Side

Blues Stay Away From Me

Cathy (melody) — Blues_____ stay a-way from me,

Linda — Blues_____ stay a-way from me,

Marcy — Blues_____ stay a-way from me,

Robin — Blues_____ stay a-way from me,

Blues_____ why don't you set me free? (I) don't know

Blues_____ why don't you set me free? (I) don't know

Blues_____ why don't you set me free?_____ (I) don't know

Blues_____ why don't you set me free? (I) don't know

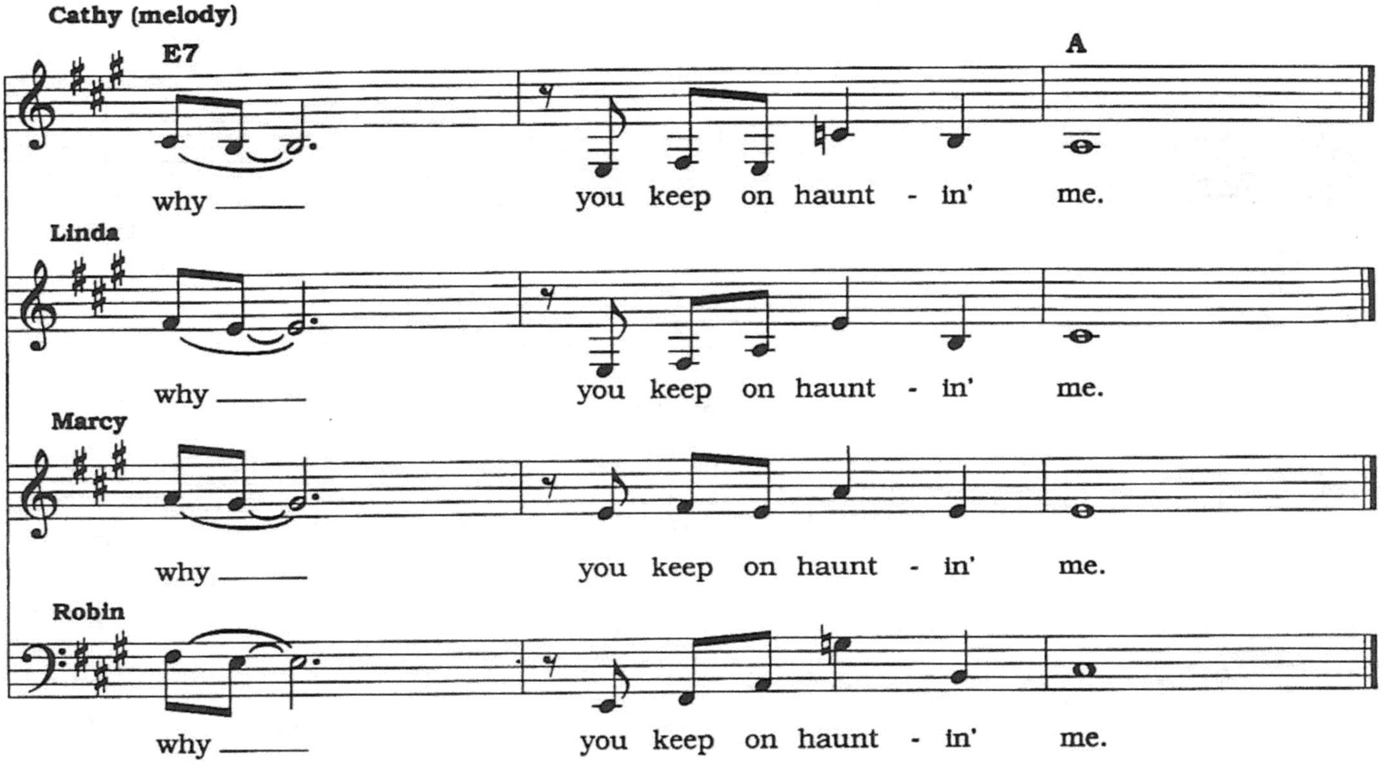

Robin's BASS RIFF

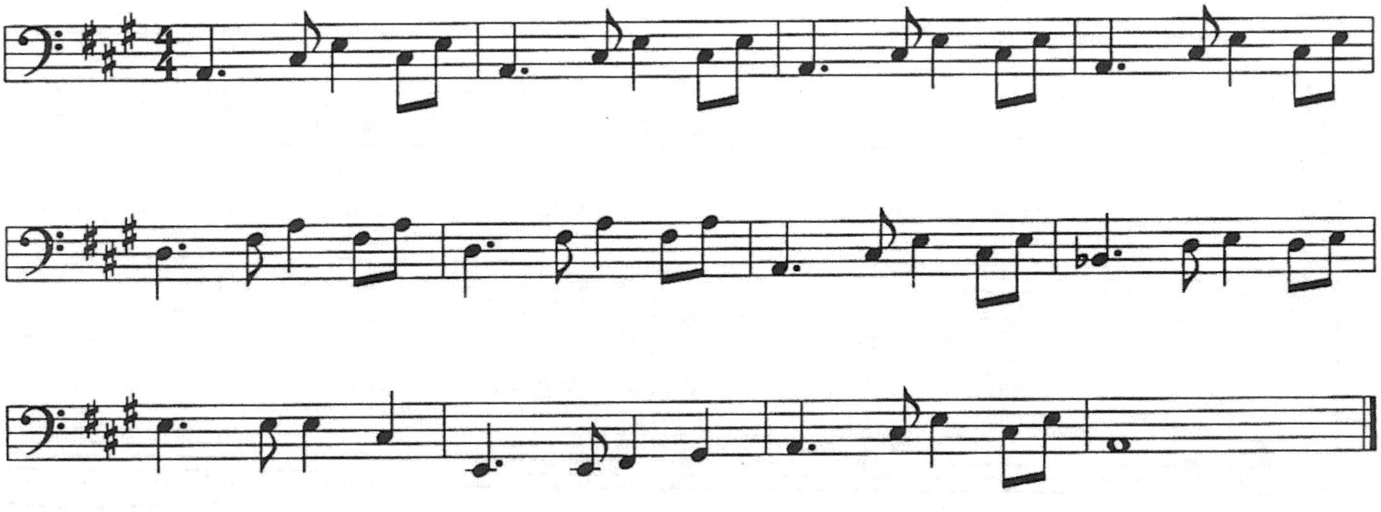

Amazing Grace

Linda
D
G
I once was lost, but now I'm
Marcy
I once was lost, but now I'm
Cathy
I once was lost, but now I'm
Robin
I once was lost, but now I'm
D
(Bm)
A
D
found, was blind but now I see.
found, was blind but now I see.
found, was blind but now I see.
found, was blind but now I see.

Irene Goodnight

Marcy
E7
A
night I - rene, good - night I - rene, I'll
Cathy
night I - rene, good - night I - rene, I'll
Linda
night I - rene, good - night I - rene, I'll
Robin
night I - rene, good - night I - rene, I'll
B7
E
see you in my dreams.
see you in my dreams.
see you in my dreams.
see you in my dreams.

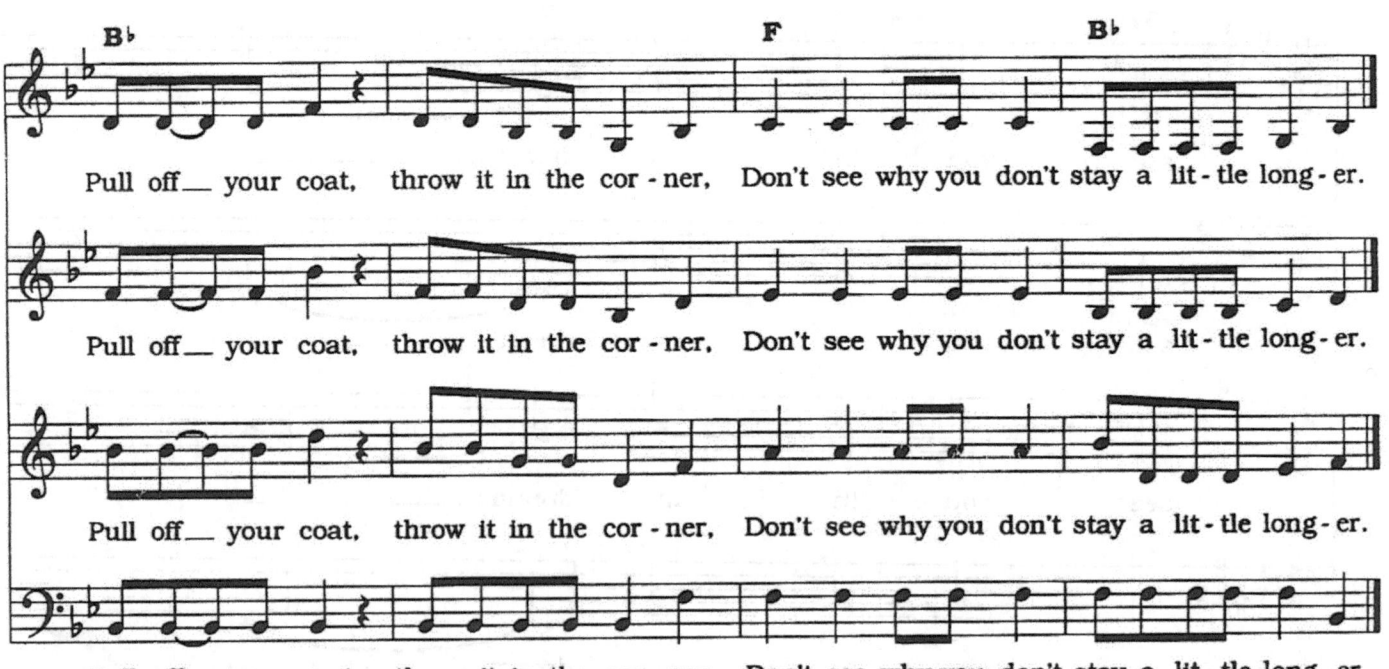

Stay All Night

Cathy: Stay all night, stay a lit-tle long-er. Dance all night, dance a lit-tle long-er.

Marcy: Stay all night, stay a lit-tle long-er. Dance all night, dance a lit-tle long-er.

Linda: Stay all night, stay a lit-tle long-er. Dance all night, dance a lit-tle long-er.

Robin: Stay all night, stay a lit-tle long-er. Dance all night, dance a lit-tle long-er.

Pull off your coat, throw it in the cor-ner, Don't see why you don't stay a lit-tle long-er.

Pull off your coat, throw it in the cor-ner, Don't see why you don't stay a lit-tle long-er.

Pull off your coat, throw it in the cor-ner, Don't see why you don't stay a lit-tle long-er.

Pull off your coat, throw it in the cor-ner, Don't see why you don't stay a lit-tle long-er.

SONG LYRICS

Gold Watch And Chain

Verse:

Darling, how can I stay here without you?
I have nothing to cheer my poor heart,
This old world would be sad, love, without you,
Tell me now that we never will part.

Keep On The Sunny Side

Verse:

Oh, the storm and its fury broke today
Crushing dreams that we cherished so dear.
Storm and cloud will in time pass away
And the sunny side will shine bright and clear.

Blues Stay Away From Me

1. Love was never meant for me.
   True love was never meant to be
   Since somehow we never can agree.

2. Life is full of misery,
   Dreams don't like the memory
   Bringing back your love that used to be.

3. Tears, so many I can't see
   Years don't mean a thing to me
   Time goes by and still I can't be free.

Amazing Grace

'Twas grace that taught my heart to fear
And grace my fears relieved
How precious did that grace appear
The hour I first believed.

Through many dangers, toils and snares
I have already come,
'Tis grace that brought me safe this far
And grace will lead me home.

Irene Goodnight

Sometimes I live in the country,
Sometimes I live in town,
Sometimes I take a great notion,
To jump in the river and drown.

Stop rambling, stop gambling,
Stop staying out late at night,
Go home to your wife and your family,
Stay there by the fireside bright.

I love Irene, God knows I do,
Love her 'til the seas run dry.
If Irene ever turns her back on me,
I'll take morphine and die.

Inscribed by CHARYLU ROBERTS

Learn to Sing Harmony

taught by Cathy Fink, Marcy Marxer, Robin and Linda Williams

Three CD lessons plus songbook

Get together with friends and create harmony parts to your favorite songs! With the help of four wonderful singer/teachers, you'll learn the principles of singing two, three, and four part harmonies to enhance your favorite country, bluegrass and folk songs. If you're a complete beginner you'll understand the theory behind harmony singing and get the ear training you'll need to develop your style. If you already have some knowledge, these CDs will help you hone your skills, increase your repertoire and gain new techniques and insights into singing with others.

The vocal parts are recorded on separate channels to allow you to try out your harmonies with Cathy, Marcy, Robin and Linda. This will give you the practice you'll need when you get together with other singers to try out your new skills. The most important thing you'll learn is that singing in harmony with others can be fun for you and your singing partners, with wonderful rewards for all who participate.

Songs:
- *Stay All Night*
- *Down By the Riverside*
- *Bury Me Beneath the Willow*
- *Broken-Hearted Lover*
- *Red River Valley*
- *Trouble In Mind*
- *Careless Love*
- *Leavin' Train*
- *Down In the Valley*
- *Turtle Dove*
- *Little Darlin' Pal of Mine*
- *Keep On the Sunny Side*
- *Blues Stay Away From Me*
- *Gold Watch and Chain*
- *Amazing Grace*
- *Goodnight, Irene*
- *I'm Going To Sit at the Welcome Table*
- *Long Journey Home*
- *Good Old Mountain Dew*
- *Hand Me Down My Walking Cane*

Cathy Fink and Marcy Marxer have been delighting audiences young and old for over twenty years. From concert halls, school assemblies and festivals to small clubs, they have inspired audiences around the world to sing. After releasing over 15 albums between them, Cathy & Marcy received their first Grammy nomination in 1997 for their album of original lullabies, Blanket Full of Dreams (Rounder) and their second in 1999 for Changing Channels (Rounder). They have won numerous awards and praise from artists and audiences alike for their tight harmony singing, songwriting and exquisite interpretations of traditional music.

For more than a quarter of a century **Robin and Linda Williams** have been performing a thoughtful and heartfelt blend of bluegrass, folk, old-time and acoustic country that truly merits the title of "American music." The duo has gained a huge following as regulars on the *Prairie Home Companion*, as well as through appearances at major folk and bluegrass festivals, clubs and community concerts. They have appeared on Nashville Network's *Fire On The Mountain*, and written and performed fourteen original songs for the theatrical production *Stonewall Country*.

Visit our website or call us for a free catalog listing hundreds of lessons on DVD and CD.

©1989, 1998 Homespun Tapes, Ltd.

Cover photo: Adam Traum

Homespun Tapes, Box 340,
Woodstock, NY 12498
845-246-2550 or 1-800-338-2737
www.homespun.com

HOMESPUN®

U.S. $37.50

HL00641533

ISBN-13: 978-0-634-04482-3
ISBN-10: 0-634-04482-6